NATIONAL GEOGRAPHIC

D0503679

Some Things Float

Lesley Pether

Some things **float**.

Some things **sink**.

What floats? What sinks?

Will this ball float?

Yes. This ball **floats**.

Will this toy float?

Yes. This toy **floats**.

Will this rock float?

No. This rock does not float.
It **sinks**.

What will sink?